Hal Leonard Student Piano Library

Notespeller for Piano

Book 1

Along the Music Trail
with Spike and Party Cat

Author
Karen Harrington

Consultants
Barbara Kreader, Fred Kern,
Phillip Keveren, Mona Rejino

Editor
Carol Klose

Illustrator
Fred Bell

FOREWORD

The **Notespeller for Piano** presents note recognition activities that coordinate with the **Piano Lessons** books in the **Hal Leonard Student Piano Library**.

Students join *Spike*, *Party Cat*, and friends as they travel along the music trail. The journey includes assignments that help students use the musical alphabet to read and write notes on the staff.

Best wishes,

Karen Harrington

ISBN 978-0-634-00477-3

HAL•LEONARD®

Visit Hal Leonard Online at
www.halleonard.com

World headquarters, contact:
Hal Leonard
7777 West Bluemound Road
Milwaukee, WI 53213
Email: info@halleonard.com

In Europe, contact:
Hal Leonard Europe Limited
1 Red Place
London, W1K 6PL
Email: info@halleonardeurope.com

In Australia, contact:
Hal Leonard Australia Pty. Ltd.
4 Lentara Court
Cheltenham, Victoria, 3192 Australia
Email: info@halleonard.com.au

Finger Numbers

Spike and Party Cat are preparing for their trip. After washing their gloves, they hang them on a line to dry. Inside each glove, write **R.H.** for right hand and **L.H.** for left hand. In the clothespin above each finger, write the finger number.

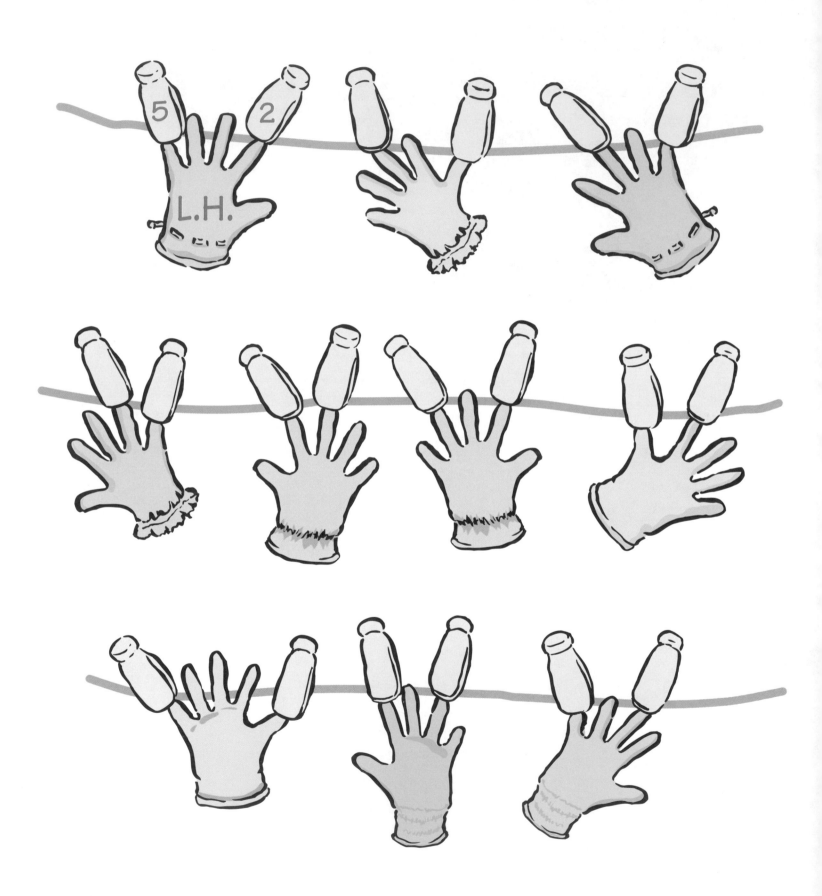

The Piano Keyboard
Twins and Triplets

Spike and Party Cat plan to visit twins and triplets.

1. Draw a blue line from each set of two black keys to the twins.

2. Draw a red line from each set of three black keys to the triplets.

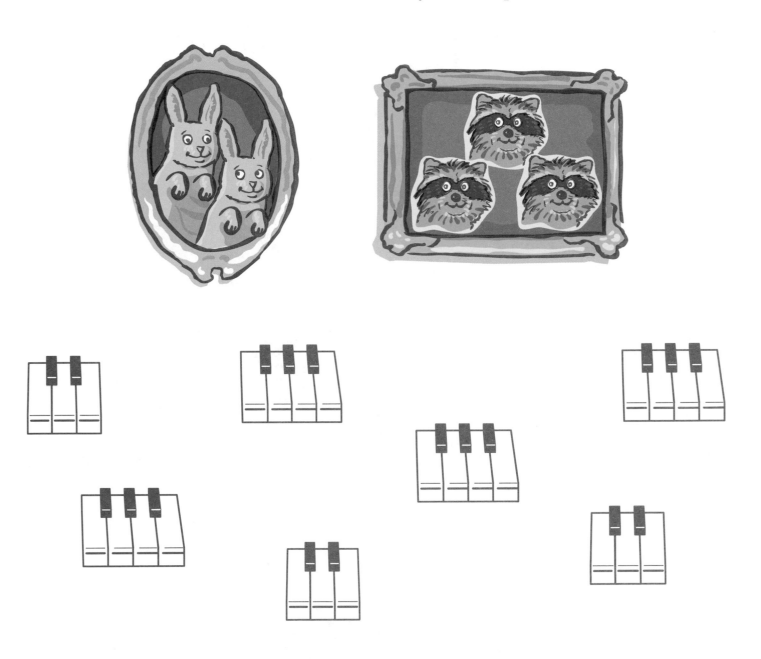

3. Color the sets of twins blue, and color the sets of triplets red.

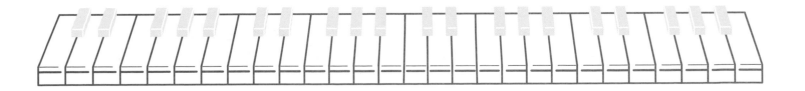

3

Step Up °°° Step Down °°° or Repeat °°°

Party Cat is trying to talk Spike into renting a canoe when they get to the river. Spike will rent the canoe if Party Cat can complete this matching game. Help Party Cat by drawing a line from each group of notes to the canoe whose oar matches the direction of the notes.

Finger Painting

Spike and Party Cat meet an artist who is painting with a different color on each finger. What fun!

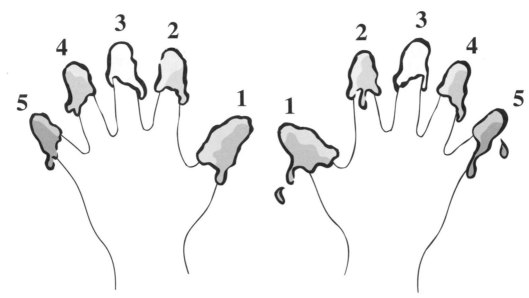

1. Circle the correct hand for each example below.
Remember, stems up = R.H., and stems down = L.H.

2. Using the colors above as your guide, write the correct finger number in the colored box below each note.

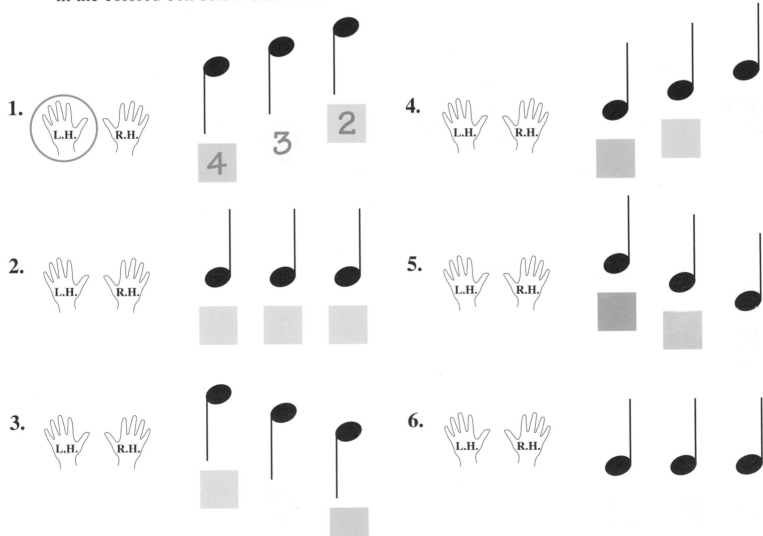

Let's Have Lunch!

Naming the White Keys

Write the name of each key on this keyboard.

Spike and Party Cat plan to have lunch at the cabin of two friends. To find out whom they will meet, begin with the first letter on each line and name the keys going up the keyboard. The letters in the blue boxes will spell their friends' names!

C ____ ____ ____ ____ ____ ____

F ____ ____ ____ ____ ____

B ____ ____ ____ ____ ____

R

and

C ____ ____ ____ ____ ____ ____

B ____ ____ ____ ____ ____

E ____ ____ ____ ____ ____

A ____ ____ ____ ____

F ____ ____ ____ ____

R

Unlock C D E !

On their journey, it's Spike's job to keep track of the keys to the bikes. Unlock the CDE groups by writing C, D, and E on the correct piano keys below.

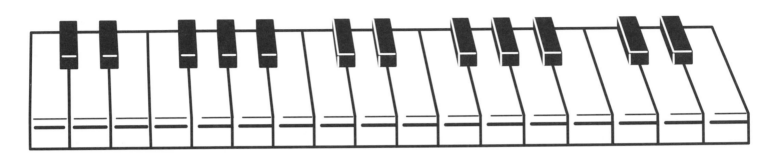

Write the key names inside the keys in this order:

1. All red keys
2. All blue keys
3. All green keys

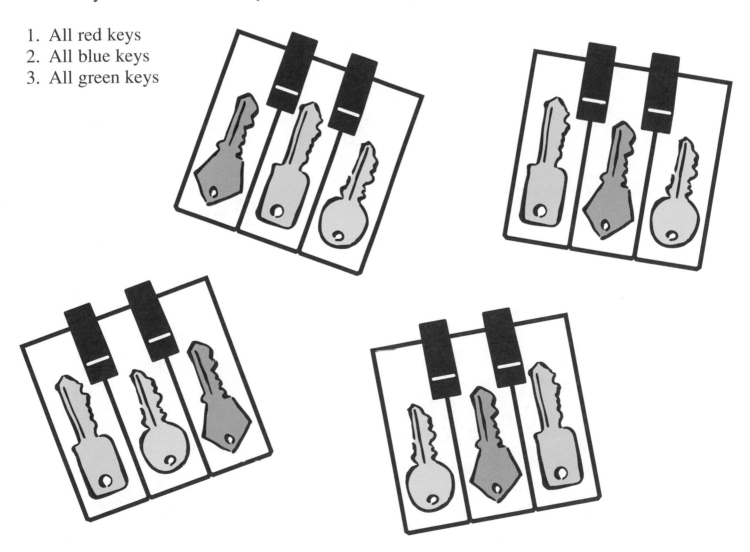

7

Use with Lesson Book 1, pg. 22

Unlock F G A B !

Unlock the F G A B groups by writing F, G, A, and B on the correct piano keys below.

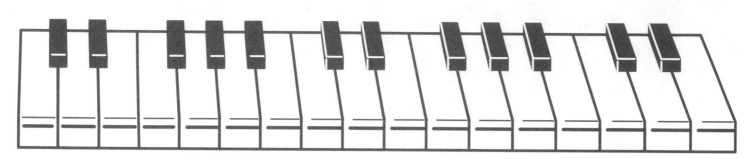

Write the key names inside the keys in this order:

1. All yellow keys
2. All purple keys
3. All orange keys
4. All brown keys

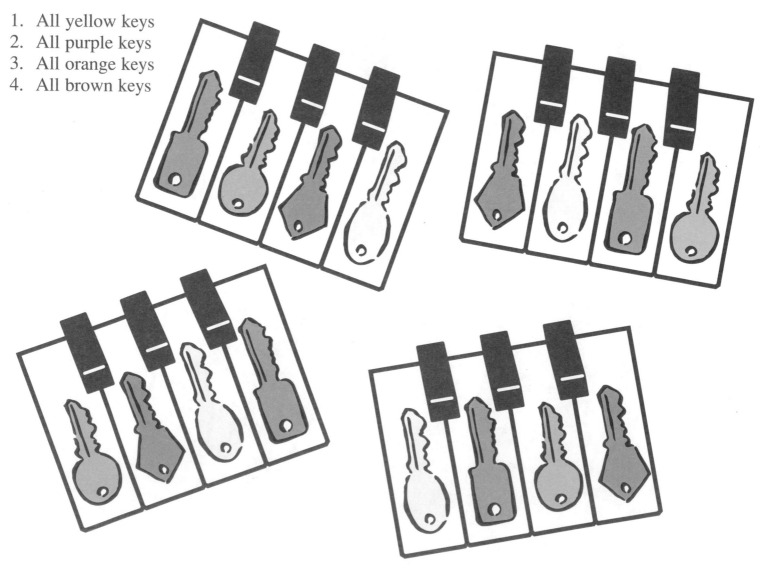

"You Lost What?"

While camping on the river, Party Cat lost something very important. This upset Spike. Begin with the letter on each line below and write the musical alphabet *backwards*. The letters in the blue boxes spell the item Party Cat lost!

A ____ ____ ____ ____ ____

F ____ ____ ____ ____

D ____ ____ ____ ____ ____

G ____ ____ ____ ____ ____

B ____ ____ ____ ____

C ____ ____ ____ ____ ____

E ____ ____ ____ ____ ____

N

O

P

L

A B C D E F G A B C D E F G A B C D E F G A B

9

Use with Lesson Book 1, pg. 25

Going Up ⟋ Going Down ⟍

During their trip, Spike and Party Cat plan to visit Spike's grandmother. They will ride an elevator up to her apartment.

1. Name the notes on the elevator *going up*.
2. Name the notes on the elevator *going down*.

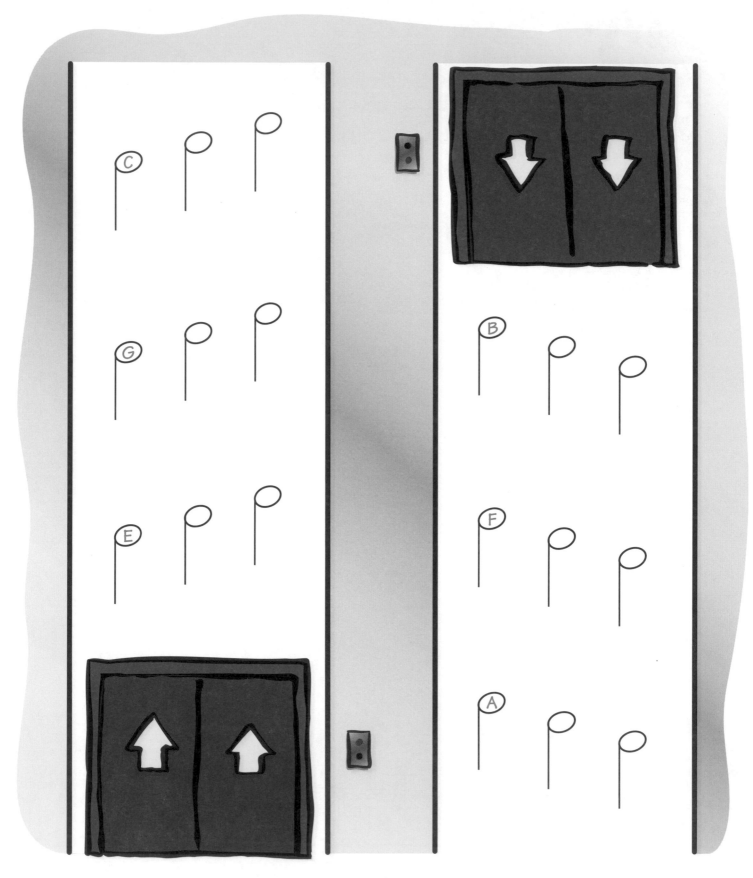

Fishing for Letter Names

Party Cat found a perfect spot for fishing on a lake.
Draw a fishing line from each piano key on the pier to the
fish with the matching letter name.

11

Line Notes and Space Notes

Line Notes

The line crosses through
the middle of the note.

Space Notes

The lines touch the top
and bottom of the note,
but do not cross through the note.

Write **L** for line note or **S** for space note in the blue boxes below.

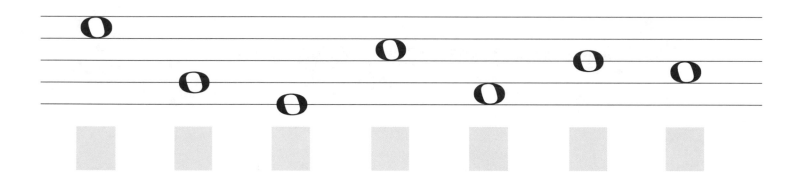

1. Trace all the line notes red.
2. Trace all the space notes blue.

Drawing Notes on Lines and Spaces

Line Numbers	Space Numbers
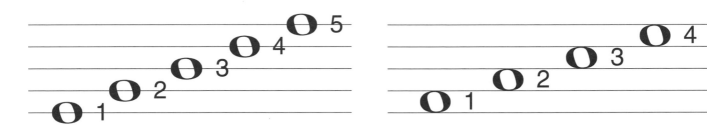

Spike and Party Cat are learning to draw notes on the lines and spaces.
Help them by following the directions below.

1. Draw whole notes through these lines:

2. Draw whole notes in these spaces:

    line 2   line 1   line 5   line 3   line 4   *space 3   space 1   space 4   space 2*

3. Draw whole notes for these lines and spaces:

line 3   space 4   space 2   line 5   line 1   line 4   space 1   space 3   line 2

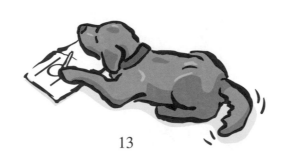

Line Up the Flags!

Spike and Party Cat are decorating their trail bikes. Spike is putting line-note flags on his bike, and Party Cat is putting space-note flags on his bike.

1. Draw a line from each *line-note* flag to the matching numbered line on Spike's bike.

2. Draw a line from each *space-note* flag to the matching numbered space on Party Cat's bike.

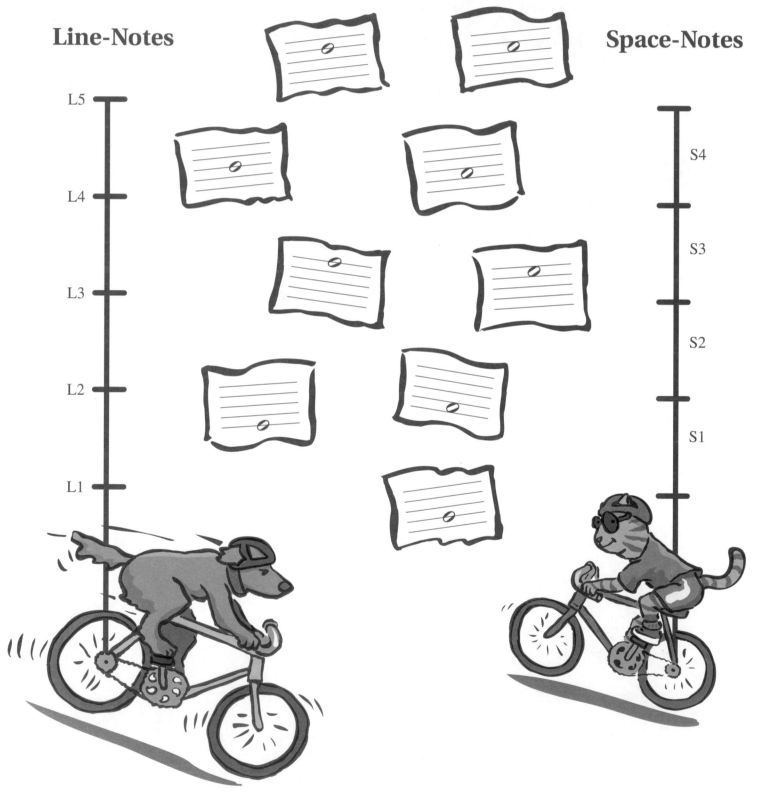

Drawing the Bass Clef Sign

If either Spike or Party Cat wants to stop
along the trail, he will hold up a Bass Clef sign.

Be a Copycat!
Copy each step to make a Bass Clef sign.

1. Draw a circle on the **F** line.

F line ⟶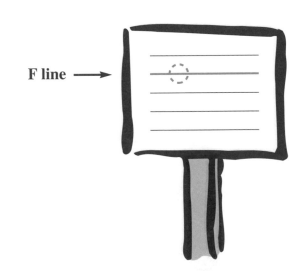

2. Draw a line curving to the right.
   Touch the top line and cross the
   2nd line.

Trace three Bass Clefs.

3. Draw two small dots, one above
   and one below the **F** line.

Draw three Bass Clefs.

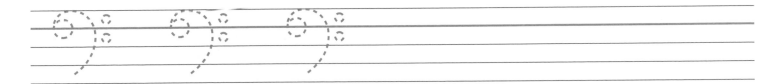

15

Use with Lesson Book 1, pg. 38

Fishes Full of F Notes

Reading Guide F

Draw four F notes.

Party Cat plans to stop along the trail to go fishing.
Circle all the **F** notes you find in the fish below.

Which fish has two **F** half-notes?

Which fish has two **F** quarter-notes?

Which fish has only one **F**?

Which fish has no **F**?

A Tall Tale

Spike enjoys telling funny stories and tall tales to his friends. Read Spike's favorite tall tale and draw a whole note on the **F** line above each **F** you find in the story.

My friend found a frog on my front fence and a fancy fine

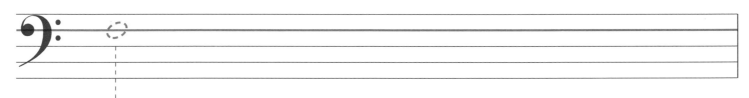

frog was he.   He did a flip flop with a fast and funny

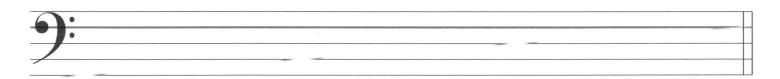

hop and off he fled to France with a fluffy little flea.

How many **F notes** did you draw?

17

Bass Clef Notes
F G A

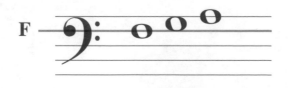

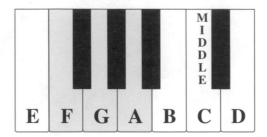

1. Write the note names in the boxes below the staff.
2. Circle the pairs of notes that repeat.

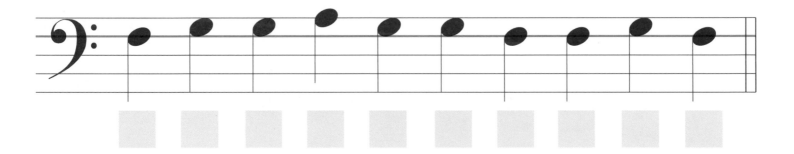

Words that begin with F, G, or A

Spike and Party Cat stop for a picnic. A few of the things they see are pictured below.

What is the first letter of each object? Draw a quarter note that has the same letter name.

Drawing the Treble Clef Sign

Spike and Party Cat are decorating
their backpacks with Treble Clef signs.

Be a Copycat!
Copy each step to make a Treble Clef.

1. Draw a straight line, ending with a hook.

2. Draw a curve down to line four.

3. Draw a curve down to line one.

4. Draw a curve up to line three, then down to the **G** line.

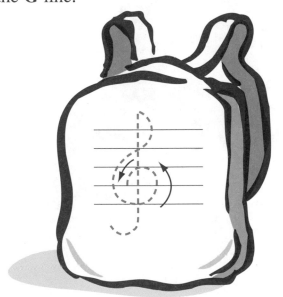

Trace three Treble Clefs.

Draw three Treble Clefs.

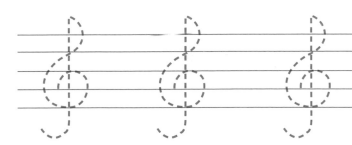

19

Gloves Full of G Notes

Reading Guide G

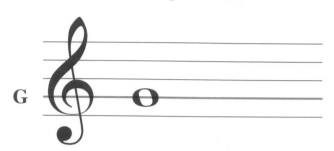

G

Draw four G notes.

While biking along the trail, Spike and Party Cat wear gloves to protect their hands. Circle all the G notes you find in the gloves below.

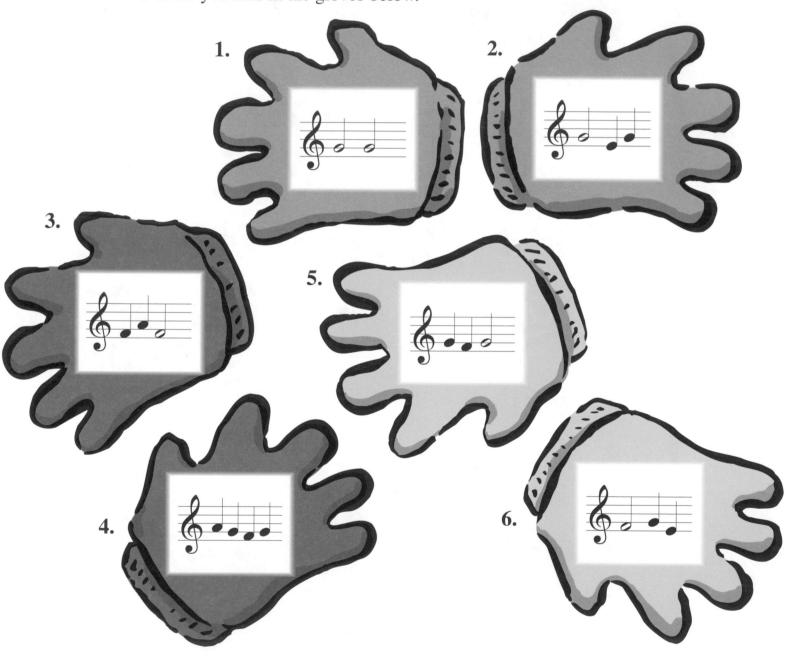

Which glove has two **G** half-notes?

Which glove has two **G** quarter-notes?

Which glove has only one **G**

Which glove has no **G**?

Meet Peggy and Gus

Along their journey, Spike and Party Cat stop to visit their friends, Peggy and Gus.
Read this rhyme and draw a whole note on the **G** line above each **G** you find.

Peggy   and   G u s   can   giggle   and   w i g g l e

and   jiggle   and   scream   while   chewing

green   gum   and   eating   ice   cream.

How many **G notes** did you draw?

21   *Use with Lesson Book 1, pg. 41*

Treble Clef Notes
E F G

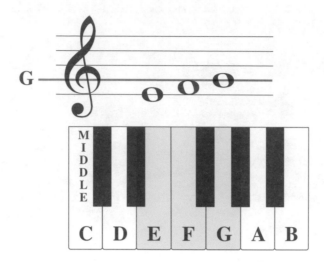

1. Write the note names in the boxes below the staff.
2. Circle the pairs of notes that repeat.

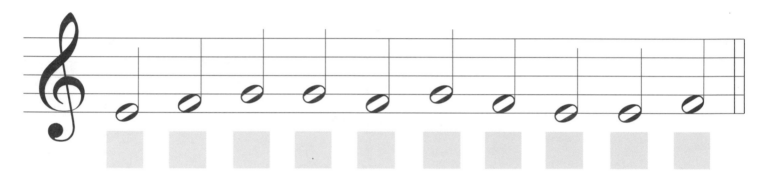

Words that begin with E, F, or G

Spike and Party Cat visit the zoo. Some of the animals they see are pictured below.

What is the first letter of each picture? Draw a half note that has the same letter name.

Hiking Up and Down

1. Draw three Middle C notes on the Treble Staff.

Reading Guide
Middle C is found between the Bass Clef and the Treble Clef.

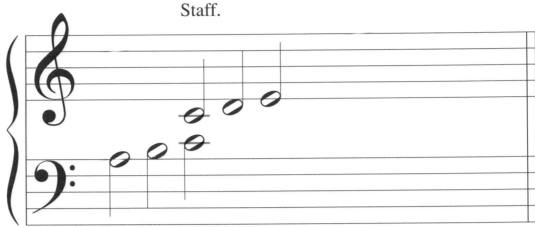

Spike and Party Cat take time to hike up and down some hills. The notes on this page step up and down like the hikers.

1. In the blue boxes below, name each note.
2. Circle the hand that should play each example.

1.
C

2.

3.

4.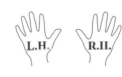

5.

6.

Use with Lesson Book 1, pg. 43

Stepping Stones

Party Cat and Spike step on stones to cross a creek.

1. Draw a half note that steps up or down from each note.
2. Write the name of each note you draw on the nearest stone.

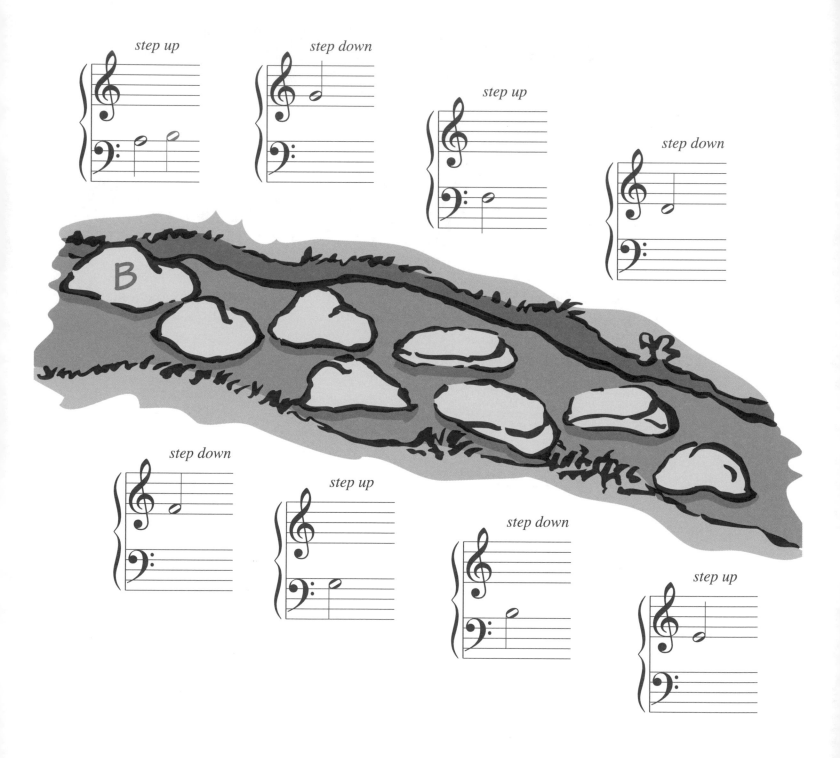

Where Is That Cat?

Party Cat is up to his tricks again!
Help Bear find him by naming these notes.

Th_ _ _t h_s _ _ _n _ _ _. H_ _t_ _ _ _r's

_ _ r _ _ l.   H_   is   hi_ _ing   with   his   f_ _ _

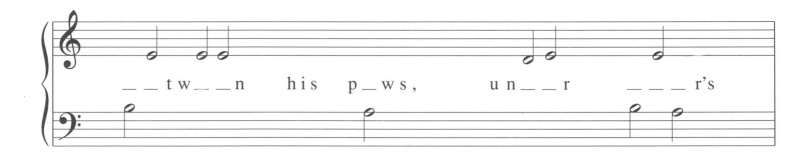

_ _tw_ _n   his   p_ws,   un_ _r   _ _ _r's

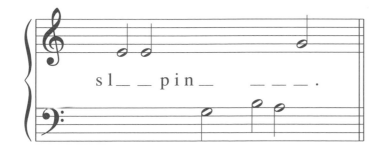

sl_ _pin_   _ _ _.

25   *Use with Lesson Book 1, pg. 45*

Safety Rules

Party Cat and Spike remember important safety rules as they have fun swimming, boating, biking, hiking, and canoeing. Match the colored boxes to the colored notes on the Grand Staff and write the correct letter name in each box.

1. Wh☐n ☐rossin☐ th☐ tr☐il, look ☐oth w☐ys.

2. W☐☐r ☐ li☐ j☐☐k☐t wh☐n you ☐re in ☐ ☐o☐t or ☐ ☐no☐.

3. N☐v☐r swim ☐lon☐.

4. Pour w☐t☐r on th☐ ☐☐mp ☐ir☐ wh☐n ☐inish☐☐.

5. Wh☐n ☐ikin☐, ☐lw☐ys w☐☐r ☐ h☐lm☐t.

Skipping on the Staff

On a pond along the trail, Spike is showing Party Cat how to skip rocks across the water.

1. Draw a line from each interval in the Skipping Up column to the same interval in the Skipping Down column.
2. In the blue boxes, name each note.

Skipping Up   **Skipping Down**

Use with Lesson Book 1, pg. 51

An Adventure on the River

Complete the story below by following these directions:

1. In the white boxes, write the letter name of each note.
2. In the blue boxes, write the letter name of the note that *skips up* or *skips down* by following the direction of the arrows.
3. Draw the skipping note on each staff.

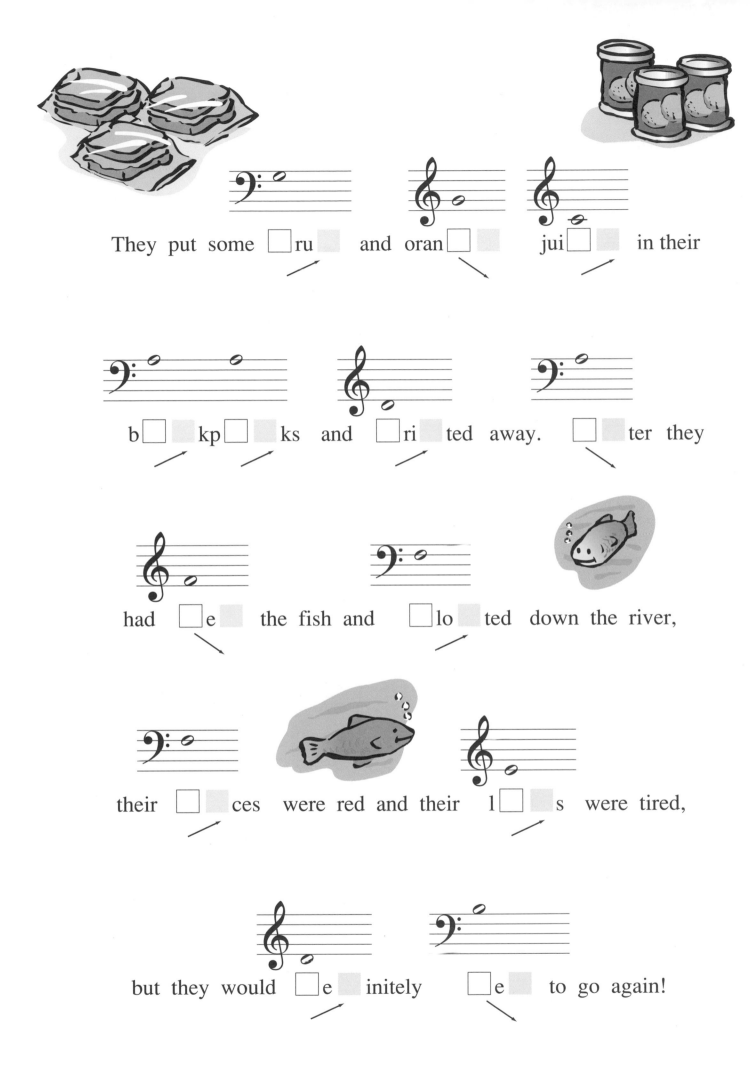

They put some ☐ru☐ and oran☐☐ jui☐☐ in their

b☐☐kp☐☐ks and ☐ri☐ted away. ☐☐ter they

had ☐e☐ the fish and ☐lo☐ted down the river,

their ☐☐ces were red and their l☐☐s were tired,

but they would ☐e☐initely ☐e☐ to go again!

Rafting Down the River

What did Spike and Party Cat see on their rafting trip?

1. In the blue boxes, write the letter names of the notes.
2. Draw a line from each note to its key on the keyboard.

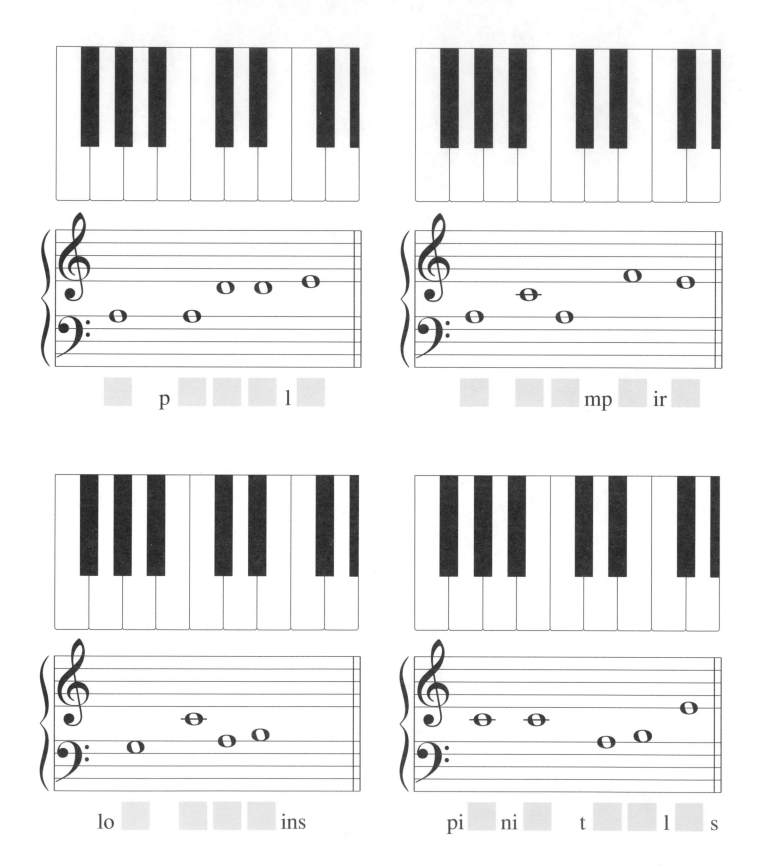

Things We Found Along the Music Trail

Below each staff is a word from Spike and Party Cat's trip along the trail.

1. In the words below each staff circle all letters that are part of the musical alphabet.
2. On the staff, draw a quarter note for each letter you circled, drawing the stems in the right direction.

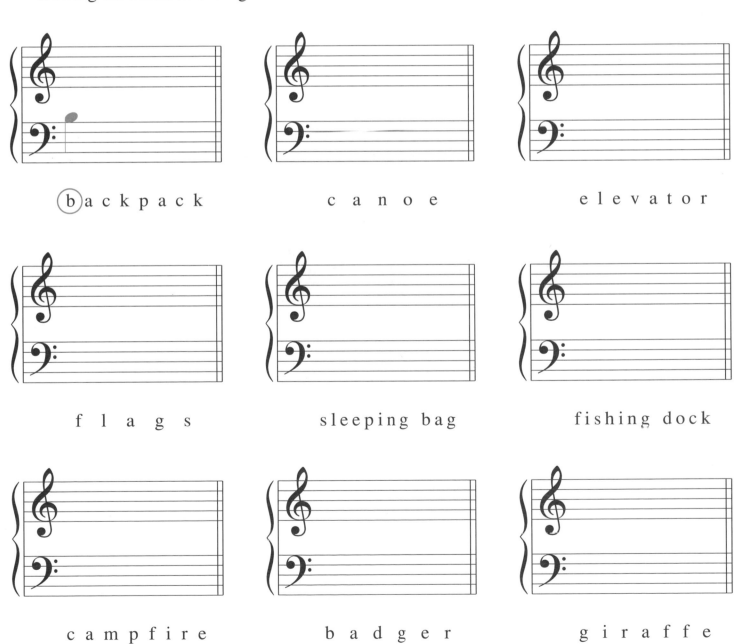

(b)ackpack

c a n o e

e l e v a t o r

f l a g s

sleeping bag

fishing dock

c a m p f i r e

b a d g e r

g i r a f f e

31

Use with Lesson Book 1, pg. 59

Campfire Memories

On the last night of their adventure, Party Cat and Spike build a campfire and roast hot dogs. They talk about the music terms they have learned along the trail. Spell these terms by naming the notes on the staffs around the campfire.